OUR CHANGING LANDSCAPE

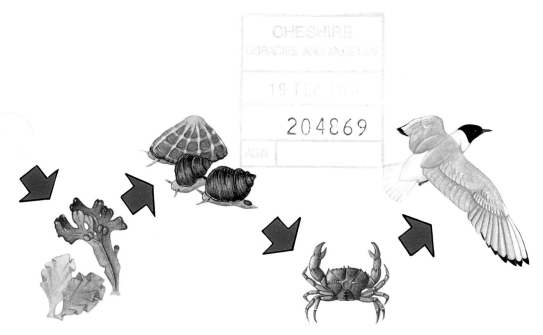

D. C. MONEY

☙ BELITHA PRESS

First published in Great Britain in 1990 by
Belitha Press Limited
31 Newington Green, London N16 9PU
Copyright © Belitha Press Limited and
Gareth Stevens, Inc. 1990
Illustrations/photographs copyright © in this
format by Belitha Press Limited and Gareth
Stevens, Inc. 1990
ISBN 1 85561 015 9
Typeset by Chambers Wallace, London
Printed in the UK for Imago Publishing
by MacLehose and Partners

British Library Cataloguing in Publication Data
CIP data for this book is available from the British
Library

Acknowledgements

Photographic credits:

N. Champion 7 bottom, 19, 40 left
The Creative Company, Milton Keynes 39
Geoscience Features 5 right
Glenrothes Development Corporation 37
Sally and Richard Greenhill 16
Susan Griggs Agency Ltd 13, 20 bottom, 47, 54
Robert Harding Picture Library 7 top, 30, 31 bottom,
    44, 52, 56, 57
The Hutchinson Library 10, 22, 23 bottom, 26, 28, 32,
    35, 41, 43 left, 46, 49
The Mansell Collection Ltd 23 top, 31 top
D C Money 4, 9, 11, 15, 18, 20 top, 25 top, 29, 33, 34,
    38, 40 right, 45, 51, 59
Marion and Tony Morrison 25 right
Joachim Schumacher 53
Science Photo Library 5 top
Spectrum Colour Library 27, 43 right
Frank Spooner Pictures 50
A. Usborne 21

Illustrated by: Nicholas Day and David Holmes
(Garden Studios), Eugene Fleury, Edward
Mortelmans (John Martins Artists)

Series editor: Neil Champion
Educational consultant: Dr Alistair Ross
Designed by: Groom and Pickerill
Picture research: Ann Usborne

Book
No.

204869

Contents

Words found in **bold** are explained
in the glossary on pages 60 and 61

1: THE CHANGING EARTH

The Earth's Surface

The stream has cut a deep gulley into the steep mountain slope in the Andes; hard rocky ledges create waterfalls. ▼

The surface of the Earth is always changing. In the lifetime of a person, most natural changes hardly seem noticeable. The familiar shapes of hills, mountains, valleys and streams seem not to alter at all. Especially when changes to the **environment** through natural forces are compared with changes brought about by people: new buildings, whole forests coming down, reservoirs made by damming rivers and wild land being tamed for farming.

Natural Forces

Sometimes natural actions can bring rapid, spectacular change. In AD 79, the volcano Vesuvius erupted. It buried the city of Pompeii in a few hours. In the western USA, during a few days in 1980, Mt. St. Helens volcano destroyed great stretches of forest and farms.

Other natural processes act very slowly, yet cause tremendous change. The earth's **crust** is divided into separate solid **plates**. Some are covered by oceans; some carry huge **landmasses**. The plates move very slowly, yet create many different landforms.

The effects of wind and water erosion

Wind-fretted face

Water-worn gulleys

Slow Changes

Where these huge plates collide, surface rocks may be gradually crumpled. Some are thrust up into mountain ranges. Where plates move apart, new oceans may spread. Where they separate, molten materials well up. Some form volcanic islands. Such processes occur over hundreds of millions of years.

The landscape is continuously changed by another process, called **erosion**. Surface rocks are buffeted by winds, cracked by frosts, worn down slowly by rainwater and rivers, and eaten into by chemicals in the air. The loosened particles fall down slopes. Running water and moving ice wear the surface and carry away the debris. In time, high mountains can be worn down.

But this is not all a process of destruction. Particles worn from rocks are spread by floods to form new soils. Some make or extend **deltas** where the river divides and flows into the sea. Others, washed into the sea, build up new rocks, which will go to form new parts of the earth's ever-changing surface.

▲ Molten material from deep beneath the surface is thrown out by explosions. Solid particles fall back to build up the volcano. Rainwater cuts gulleys into the loose material of the volcanic core.

▲ Oalui Island is the top of a volcano built up from the Pacific Ocean bed, deep down. Notice how other small cones have been formed by later eruptions and the crater forming a circular inlet in the foreground.

◄ Rivers carry particles of worn rock, which form islands and deltas when deposited at the mouth. ▼

Sediment   Small islands formed by sediment

River flowing to sea

Sea

Delta

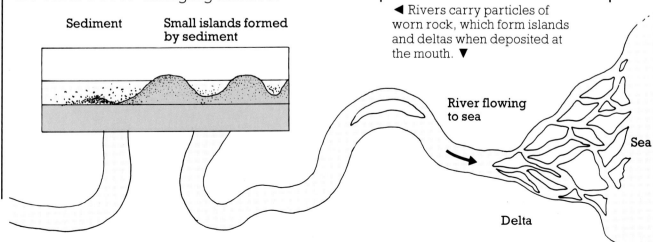

Change

Early human settlements had simple requirements to ensure their survival: fresh water, forests, a stable supply of animals to hunt for food and clothing and, later, fertile soils for them to grow crops. ▶

Ten thousand years ago most people lived in small groups, scattered over the earth. Their ways of life were adapted to their natural environment. If they upset the natural balance of forest or grassland, or used up water resources, they were forced to move on to find new places to live.

In time, these **communities** settled where there was water, **fertile** soils, and building materials. Centres of civilisation developed

The rate of growth for early settlements was generally slow. Populations did not grow rapidly, due to a high mortality rate. But as the communities did develop, they would tame the land around them. This would include cutting down forests, cultivating bigger areas, bridging rivers and expanding on the other bank and making paths useful for hunting or trading with other communities. ▶

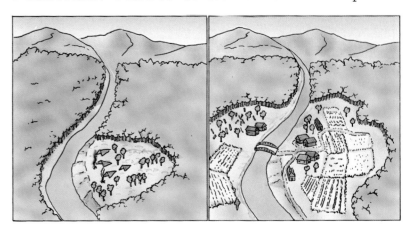

along river valleys, such as the Nile in Egypt, Euphrates in Iraq, Indus in Pakistan, and Huang He in China. Some flourished amid mountains like the Andes.

Houses, fields, workshops, roads and water channels changed the landscape. People learned to use the energy of animals, water and fuels. So changes were rapid. Woodland was destroyed to provide charcoal. The Earth's surface was broken to provide minerals.

▲ The Indus Valley, Ladakh, in Northern India. The River Indus was at the centre of one of the earliest great civilisations. Its wide, fertile banks provided food for a great many people. It flows through what are today Pakistan and India.

◀ The ruins of Rome amongst modern buildings. Once one of the ancient world's most splendid and powerful cities. It grew up from earliest times on the banks of the River Tiber, in Italy, and became the centre of a great Empire.

Pressure on the Land

Our ability to change the landscape has increased. A hundred years ago travel between countries could take days or even weeks. They now have instant links by telephone, radio, and television. Inventions spread rapidly. More people are finding new ways of changing our environment. Now *five thousand million* of us use more land for farms, factories and cities.

Long-term Effects

Sadly, we do not always consider the future. We suffer from our own chemical and radioactive **pollution**. We destroy many **plant** and animal **species**. Not just trees and large animals; but minute creatures that can affect the whole balance of life about them.

The things we destroy affect other resources. Forest removal does not just destroy species we should preserve: it can affect the whole **atmosphere**, even the outer atmosphere, which controls Earth's temperatures.

Changing for the Better

The world's population continues to grow. People change the landscape to improve living standards. We use new knowledge to try to produce enough food for the thousands of millions of people in the world. Though we have not yet learned to distribute it evenly.

Living standards have risen, though more for some than others. The **life expectancy** for China's thousand million people has risen from 35 years to 68 in less than half a century!

This illustration shows, in three stages, the same piece of land used differently over the centuries. The first shows a castle and village in the Middle Ages; the second, nineteenth century factory development; the third, modern high-rise flats, golf course and light industry. ▶

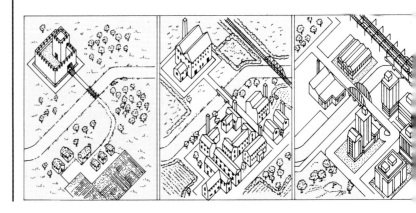

Crowds make their way to work in Xian City in Northern China. When Xian was the ancient capital of China the people lived within the walls, whose gate you see towering up at the end of the road. Now millions live here. Factories spread far beyond the walls (notice the chimneys), and flats and offices are jammed in between the small homes and shops. ◄

We shall now look at the ways in which people interact with their environment, and how we can keep a watch on the results. We will consider separately various human activities: farming, industry, developing towns and cities, communications, and so on, and how they continue to change our landscapes.

▲ At Queenstown amid the beautiful forests of Western Tasmania sulphur fumes from copper smelters have destroyed the vegetation, and water erodes the bare hillsides.

9

2: THE ENVIRONMENT

Upsetting the Balance

Everywhere living and non-living things affect one another. Plants use energy from the sun (**solar energy**) to develop. Animals obtain energy by eating plants, or each other.

Solar energy heats rocks and soils, which warm the air above. It thus affects the weather. **Weathering** breaks up surface rocks. Their particles form the soils upon which plants grow. Water dissolves the minerals in the soil and these are drawn up by the plants.

Sunlight enables plants to store energy. It allows leaves to take water and carbon dioxide from the air to build into **carbohydrates**. The leaves may be eaten by animals or they will eventually fall and tiny organisms (bacteria) will rot them down. This releases minerals back into the soil. Animal manure also returns minerals to the soil.

Tropical rainforests are very special and fragile environments. They are teeming with plant and animal life all of which depends upon the protection of the trees. When these are removed, as they are being in huge numbers, soil is washed away in floods and the land becomes barren. ▶

A food chain

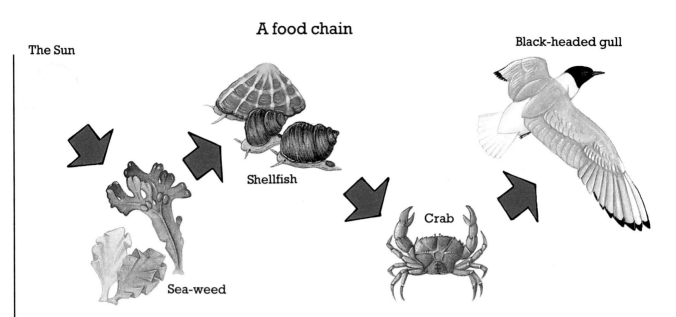

The Sun

Sea-weed

Shellfish

Crab

Black-headed gull

We call such a system an **ecosystem**, from the Greek word *eco*, which means 'a household'. Any change, say a lack of water, can affect all members of the natural system.

Natural Habitats

The balance of a natural community also depends on competition. Small plants grow in the shade of taller ones. Vines, seeking light, twist upward about trees. Birds roost high up. Reptiles and mammals seek safe hiding places, or space to move quickly.

Natural happenings alter the balance: some suddenly, like floods or volcanic eruptions: others slowly, like the gradual vegetation changes that come with the warmer conditions following an ice age.

When the climate changes, it can disturb the balance. Lengthy drought can turn dry grassland to desert. Then in wetter periods the vegetation will grow again. Unfortunately, people may prevent the plants from recovering. For instance, in the dry grasslands south of the Sahara Desert, herdsmen slowly move cattle over pastures greened by summer rain; but when the rains fail, their numerous animals over-graze the sparse vegetation. They trample and loosen dry soils. When reliable rain returns, parts of the grassland do not recover: people have extended the desert.

▲ Energy from the sun is used by the sea-weeds; it passes to the shellfish, whose flesh supplies energy for the crab. The sea-birds receive energy from a variety of plants and shore-dwelling animals.

Cattle grazing the dry brown landscape near Mekele in Ethiopia will return to these walled compounds. Straw stacked from the harvest must last until the rains come. If the rains fail, cattle and people may starve. ▼

11

Living in Harmony

The Mayans

The Mayan civilization flourished from about AD 300 to AD 900. They were very advanced in terms of their picture writing and numbering system. They even had a calendar. But they had not learned how to use metals, nor had they invented the wheel.

Some communities have scarcely disturbed the natural balance. The Mayan Indians, who lived in the Central American forests for thousands of years, changed little over the centuries. Families built riverside houses thatched with leaves. They gathered roots, fruits and wild honey. They hunted deer, wild pig, turkey and pheasant. Streams provided fish, snails and crabs.

Contacts with the Spanish conquerors were few. They learned to plant corn, beans and citrus fruit. But this hardly affected the forest. They cleared and burnt undergrowth and trees. For a while the ash fertilised the soil. When crop yields fell, they cleared an area nearby. Forest re-covered the old clearing; though there was a new balance between plants.

The arrival of Spanish conquistadores brought an end to Amer-Indian control over their own destinies. Horses, armour and weapons gave the small Spanish forces the power to conquer. ▶

12

Traditional Indian Ways

About a hundred years ago outsiders began to fell **mahogany** trees. Others cut into **sapodilla** trees to get chicle fluid for chewing gum. They set up camps and fouled the streams.

More recently, people came from the overcrowded highlands of southern Mexico. They cleared huge areas for farms, ranches, roads and airstrips. Yet many farms failed. There was no forest vegetation to replace minerals removed by crops.

The Mexican Maya Indians are now confined to 'natural forest parks'. They live in tin-roofed shacks. They no longer hunt, but get canned foods from nearby townships. Tourists look for 'traditional Indian ways'. Sadly these no longer exist. The former balance between people and environment can never return.

▲ The Amer-Indian peoples of Central America lived in their own organised societies. For their ceremonies, labourers and craftsmen helped to create immense stone structures like that you see here.

A Mayan Indian family burn branches to cook tortillas. Their home and furniture are built from forest materials, but now their dresses are brought from a local store. ◄

13

Changing the Landscape

The steep roof of this Swiss house sheds the snow. Traditionally, the family lives in the upper storey. Animals, housed and fed beneath, are kept near the farm in the winter months. ▼

Elsewhere, settlers have successfully changed the landscape. They have skilfully replaced natural vegetation with crops and settlements. For example, terraces have been cut into hillsides and been carefully maintained for hundreds of years. Rice seedlings have replaced forest plants. A balance is preserved; though not the natural one.

Skill alone is not enough for success. Heat, moisture and volcanic soils allow the Balinese to make the landscape productive. By contrast, many Ethiopian families get a bare living from their volcanic soils. The rainfall and water supplies are unreliable. Their possessions are few. A landscape reflects what nature offers and what people are capable of, in the circumstances.

Increasing Population

Old settlements often blend with the environment. Villages can seem almost part of the mountainside. The house tells of a rural life.

Small communities are concerned with what surrounds them, and until recently this was true of most market towns. But the world's population is rapidly increasing and food must now travel quickly from place to place. Most people now live in the cities and are no longer in touch with a changing countryside.

▲ The fertile volcanic slopes of the Ayung river valley in Bali have been cleared of forest and terraced to give flat surfaces for rice growing.

◄ In Ethiopia small fields follow the contours of volcanic slopes leading down to a dry winding river-course.

The acid rain cycle

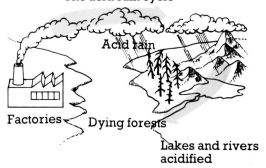

Acid rain

Factories

Dying forests

Lakes and rivers acidified

Polluted Landscapes

Goods are mass-manufactured to supply these huge populations. Raw materials may come from distant places. All of which can harm the landscape.

Manufacturing can also release harmful substances into the air. West winds carry acids from British factories and power stations across the North Sea. In Scandinavian forests trees are dying. Pond life is being destroyed. There may be other causes; but **acid rain** water is certainly harmful.

Rates of change

Our ability to change the landscape shows how careful we should be. Earth-moving equipment can destroy countryside in a matter of hours; the explosives do so in seconds. But the effects of acid rain slowly increase, at first unnoticed. Once destroyed, the natural plant and animal life can never be fully restored.

15

3: FARMING

Types of Farming

Farming has greatly changed the world's landscapes. At first people hunted and gathered leaves, grains, roots and fruits from many different wild plants. When they began to rear animals and to cultivate plants, they selected those types that suited them best. They concentrated on those best suited to local conditions. People simplified the natural plant and animal communities.

This is the basis for most farming today. In a wheatfield, a farmer removes other plants that interfere with the crop. People have hand-weeded or **harrowed** the soil since farming began. Now chemical sprays are used to kill unwanted plants. The crop is nourished by fertilisers.

Similarly, grasses, clovers and other fodder plants are chosen to suit flocks and herds. Others are removed, as far as possible. Far-

Today, huge combine harvesters work in teams to get grain from the huge wheatfields of Kansas, U.S.A., which were once natural open prairie land. ▼

mers breed only those animals that provide what people like: special pigs for lean bacon, for example.

Farming just one crop can be dangerous. It goes on removing the same soil minerals. As these become scarce, the crop fails. So farmers rotate crops. A wheat crop that removes nitrogen salts is followed by one, like beans or clover, that puts them back; or by pasture, for animal manure fertilizes the soil. Artificial fertilizers may be used, but they are expensive, and need careful control.

Insect pests carry diseases caused by **viruses** that attack the single crop. These pests must be destroyed by **pesticides** that are often too expensive, and may harm water sources. In time, some pests will no longer be killed by the pesticides.

Energy for Farming

Successful farming needs various kinds of energy. There is the sun's energy, and that of labourers and draught animals, such as mules and bullocks. There is fuel to power machinery or drive pumps. Running water or wind are used to turn wheels, and so generate electricity. Energy is used in making fertilizers and pesticides.

Crop rotation

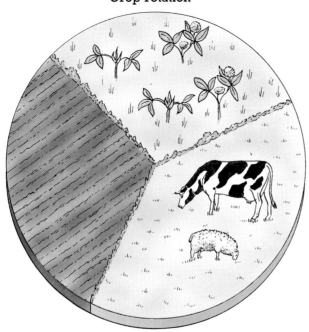

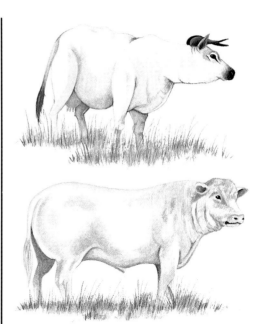

▲ Native cattle and sheep are carefully bred to produce the qualities we need – heavy beefcattle or heavy wool-bearing sheep.

◄ Harvesting removes nitrogen from the field; lucerne or clover put it back, as do the droppings of animals: so land-use is rotated – each field sown to grain every three years.

17

Farming and Planning

The hill country of south-west England has been changed by hedges to enclose some pastures and fodder crops. Old farmhouses and their storage barns form a small community in the shelter of the valley. ▼

The farming landscape depends partly on natural conditions and partly on how people are organised. Some own land and modern equipment. Some form **collective groups**, who farm together and share the benefits. Millions of peasant farmers rent land, paying cash or part of their produce. They farm mainly to supply their families. They use family labour with, perhaps, a draught animal.

Some live in country that is difficult to farm. Others farm flat fertile land and can produce enough to sell even with simple equipment.

In countries like Egypt, India and China, patterns of fields and villages have developed over thousands of years. In fertile areas, they make up the whole rural landscape. Even in countries like England, past patterns remain.

How people organise *themselves* also affects the landscape. In China, a family, or group of villagers, agree to cultivate a particular area, and to sell a certain amount to the State. They use the land well, for they can sell any extra for their own profit. Groups often combine to buy and share equipment.

Farming Economics

Water affects all farming patterns. Even where it is plentiful, it must be carefully controlled.

Dry areas may need irrigation. Shortages even affect developed countries. In eastern England many crops depend on spray irrigation. This is expensive so the farmer must sell his produce at high prices.

A wealthy population can afford high prices. So farmers increase yields by using fertilisers, pesticides and irrigation. This is **intensive farming**. The landscape may include greenhouses producing vegetables, or **factory farms** with hundreds of pigs, or thousands of **battery hens**.

▲ In developed countries, farmers can afford to hire aircraft to spray fertilisers or pesticides on their land.

The level valley floor amid the mountains of North Wales has enclosed grassy pastures for sheep near the isolated farmhouse. During summer, controlled by sheepdogs, they find grazing on the hillslopes. ▼

Farming for Profit

Modern farming in Cyprus ▼ produces fruit and vegetables for tourists' demands, using plastic cloches, a forest of wind pumps, trucks, tractors and fertilisers – a large input of energy.

Woolly Facts

● Australia provides about 25 per cent of the world's wool supply.

● People have used wool as a fabric for making clothing for over 12,000 years.

● Australia has around 160 million sheep – about 10 times as many as the people who live there.

Fencing and pumped water supplies transformed huge areas of Australian outback from the habitat of native animals, like the kangaroo, into stations (farms) supporting many thousands of sheep. ▶

The farmer runs a business. The countryside works like a well-organised factory producing crops and livestock for which there is a market (what people want and will buy). Farmlands have different patterns. In some, crops and pastures are rotated between one field and another. But some regions are best suited to animal grazing; others to crops grown in large, open fields.

Some countries export large quantities of grain, meat and wool. About a hundred years ago, European settlers in America and Australia converted immense stretches of the natural grasslands to grain and stock farming. Vast areas of the Argentine pampas were sown with grasses and clovers. In Australia, dry grassland and tree scrub were cleared for sheep and wheat farming.

On the American prairies blocks of land close to the railways were granted to pioneer farmers. Roads soon bordered these properties. This pattern of settlement remains.

Exporting

Most of the produce went to Europe's growing population. Grain stored in dockside **elevators** was shipped in bulk. Ships carried meat in refrigerated store rooms.

This **extensive farming** relied on natural grassland soils. Yields were never as high as in Western Europe, but such large areas could produce a great bulk of grain. However, as the soils became less fertile, yields fell and now fertilisers are often sprayed from aircraft.

Mechanical equipment, from horse-drawn ploughs to combine-harvesters, has always been used. Teams of harvesters with modern machines move from farm to farm. In Australia, teams of shearers travel from one property to another. Few people work permanently on one farm.

These landscapes now have large farms, isolated homesteads and straight roads and railways connecting them to collecting points and ports.

▲ A farmer in Northern Italy checks rice grown by modern intensive methods before it is exported to Scandinavia. A Scandinavian family (top) far from a rice-growing environment serves rice imported from Italy.

21

Plantations

In other countries, demand for a certain product has changed the landscape. Plantations produce a single crop on a large scale. For two centuries tropical plantations have provided the produce that Western Europe and North America need but cannot grow: cotton for textiles; latex, from rainforest trees, for rubber; coffee, tea, tobacco, cocoa and sugar-cane as luxuries for the richer industrial nations. Huge areas of the tropics were planted with billions of seedlings and cuttings.

On plantations, rows of carefully tended crops have replaced natural vegetation. There are processing factories, houses for management and workers, roads and railways to collect and distribute the produce.

In some countries there are large areas under a single crop: for instance, mulberries grown for silkworms, an age-old form of agriculture in China. Today, silk and textile factories form part of the Chinese landscape.

Places such as California, with a Mediterranean climate, produce oranges, lemons and grapefruit on estates run as businesses. Skilled employees operate machinery and processing equipment.

Many places have large, highly organised vineyards for the production of grapes for wine. Vines need continuous, careful treat-

Women picking leaves on a tea plantation. Tea plantations are found in several countries of the world, including India, Sri Lanka and China. ▼

ment. There is crushing equipment, wine storage areas, machine sheds and offices.

Farming changes the landscape in many ways. Some methods cause great damage. As with any ecosystem, a successful balance must be achieved between what nature provides and what people put in and take out.

▲ A 19th century cotton plantation on the banks of the Mississippi river. Picked cotton is taken direct to the factory for cleaning and ginning. In the foreground, animal carts carry cotton bales and beyond is a steamboat used for wider transportation.

◄ Row after row of carefully tended orange trees show the huge scale of 'factory farming' in California, U.S.A.

4: SETTLEMENTS

Market Settlements

Natural advantages

Some towns have grown more than others. In hilly country, roads must follow valleys. Where valleys meet is a good place to have a trading centre. The actual site depends on local conditions such as freedom from floods, or protection by natural features. Early market towns had to guard their growing wealth. Building on top of a hill or in the bend of a river gave some protection. Durham, in north-east England, lies above a deep-cut loop of the river Wear; so it had both these advantages.

This community has developed where there are natural geographical advantages. ▼

In a long-settled rural landscape we find a pattern of villages and towns. As the population increases towns become bigger and spread out over the countryside. Some become cities.

Living in Towns

There are many reasons why people have chosen to live in settlements. A site may have offered protection, or reliable water, or minerals. But even where families were scattered over rich farmland, villages developed, often as markets.

Through the ages families farmed mainly to feed and clothe themselves. But at times they would have more grain, vegetables, **hides**, or wool than they needed. So they looked for neighbours who had goods to exchange. Instead of travelling from one to another, it suited them all to bring their produce to a convenient centre. So daily, weekly, or seasonal markets developed.

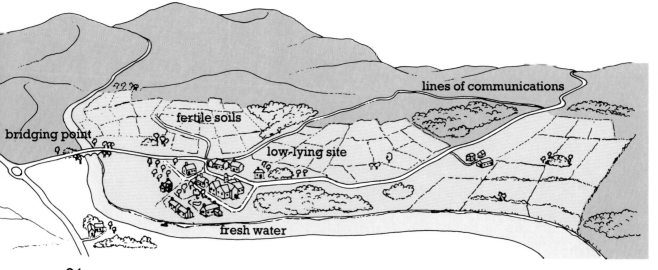

lines of communications

fertile soils

bridging point

low-lying site

fresh water

Market Towns

Rural landscapes all over the world include small market towns. At the busy market people make a living by offering services: they sell food and drink, or repair vehicles. Craftsmen, such as potters, carpenters and blacksmiths, make and sell their wares and services. They build small shops and houses for their families. The town becomes larger.

A large well-sited market town comes to have inns, banks and local government offices. People like doctors and lawyers are attracted. Their families and employees swell the population. So the settlement spreads.

This pattern of villages and market towns is found in fertile lowlands in many countries, in eastern China, in northern India, in Western Europe. It also developed on the American prairies, even though land was sold and settled in large blocks.

Industrial Growth

Some towns have grown because of a particular industry: textile towns in New England, USA; steel towns like Sheffield, in northern England. But most towns have factory districts. They also have service industries employing shopworkers, teachers, postmen and so on. Work places, like houses, are part of the urban landscape.

▲ A small market town in southwest China, where families from nearby villages bring in surplus produce or hand-made goods for sale.

The central market in Cuzco city in the Peruvian Andes, crowded on a festival day. ▼

25

Inside a Town

The car enables people to travel to where clusters of suburban shops, or large shopping centres, provide services and convenience goods for daily use. ▶

As we travel through a large town, the landscape changes. There is a business centre with large shops and offices. Few basic foods, clothing, and household goods are now produced locally. They are delivered by truck to shops. One company may own shops in many different towns. Such shops, selling many different goods, group together near the town centre. So people find what they want in a small area.

Close by are banks, insurance companies and government offices, serving both businesses and shoppers. Here land is expensive, so buildings tend to be tall to take up less space on the ground. Part of the old centre may survive. In many European towns, this may include a church, castle ruins, and an old inn, for instance.

Housing is often a problem in the centre of a large town. Many people prefer to live outside the town. Large old houses in the centre become shabby flats in order to squeeze in more people. There is often much poverty.

From Inner City to Suburbs

As the city becomes even bigger the old inner town gives way to spreading **suburbs**, with shopping centres, schools, and parks of their own. The city centre is too far for daily shopping, and so groups of small shops or mini-markets spring up. On main highways and ring roads large covered shopping centres with car parks may be found. These offer both daily supplies and things like furniture and electrical goods. There are often travel firms and banks.

New housing is built on the outskirts of the city. Industrial estates with new factories and warehouses are sited near ring roads, so that transport avoids the city centre. A city thus develops a landscape pattern of its own.

▲ The modern city of Athens, where shops and offices, and tall apartment blocks cluster about the ancient Acropolis, and dense suburban housing spreads to the shore and far away inland.

Spreading Cities

The squalor of self-built shacks which form shanty towns about the modern high-rise buildings of São Paulo, Brazil. At first they lack sanitation, electricity and piped water, but as housing is improved the authorities may supply these and create outward-spreading suburbs. ▼

Less industrially developed countries also have a rapidly growing population. Peasant farmers cannot get more land. Sometimes the land is divided. Fields become smaller and cannot support a growing family. There are seldom enough jobs in villages and small towns. So people leave for the larger towns and cities. Droughts or floods in rural areas can cause thousands to flee to the cities.

As rural families move in, they add to the overcrowding in the cities. They cannot easily find housing or work. Many build shacks on waste land on the edge of the city. These squatter, or 'shanty', areas lack piped water, electricity and proper sanitation. There are few large factories, so newcomers seek jobs such as carrying, cleaning, or selling small items in the street.

City Centres and Squatter Suburbs

The sprawling cities of the less developed countries have different landscapes. Many have business centres set up by Europeans in colonial times. Their large buildings, wide

◀ In over-populated cities like São Paulo young people of immigrant families sell matches, clean shoes, or carry loads, hoping in time to find better-paid work.

streets, squares and parks remain. Beyond are crowded narrow streets with small shops. Old buildings house many families. There are often bustling street markets. Wealthier suburbs have more space. But, even within the city, squatters occupy waste land.

On the outskirts are shanty settlements. In time some may develop into proper suburbs. As people improve their housing, the government may provide water and electricity.

Squatter housing on the outskirts of Asunción City in Paraguay is gradually being improved. So, gradually, proper suburbs spread out from the main city. ▼

The New Industrial Countries

This 'super-express' train can travel from Tokyo at 220 kph (140 mph) over the lines linking the many industrial cities of south-east Japan. ▼

Several old **colonial ports** now have strikingly different landscapes. Ocean trade routes, commerce and banking have brought great wealth to Hong Kong and Singapore. They encourage small industries. They export huge quantities of clothing, electrical and electronic goods. Office blocks tower above business centres. Families live in closely packed high-rise flats.

Planning Urban Growth

China, too, has different urban landscapes. Eight hundred million Chinese live in rural areas. But few will migrate to a city to avoid overcrowding there.

Some cities, like Beijing and Shanghai, include the countryside for hundreds of kilometres around them. They govern the small towns and villages that supply the main city with food, and set up new towns to provide jobs away from the crowded city.

◀ British ships anchored off Hong Kong Island, off China's Pearl river estuary in the mid-nineteenth century. The island overlooking this strategic harbour was acquired by Britain by treaty in 1842; Kowloon, in the foreground, became British in 1861; and in 1898 New Territories stretching inland were leased until 1997 (when the People's Republic of China regains it all).

Light industries are encouraged in China's country towns. They provide goods and jobs for local people. So rural towns become larger, rather than the cities.

By contrast, in the eastern USA and Japan railways and motorways link almost continuous industrial cities. Huge urban areas consume large amounts of energy. But energy is scarce in the poorer countries. It is difficult to improve urban living standards without it.

Today modern high-rise commercial, industrial buildings and flats line Hong Kong Island's western shore (seen above). Along the harbour, beyond Kowloon (top, right) ocean ships lie off the container docks and heavy industrial zones on the mainland. ▼

5: COMMERCE AND INDUSTRY

Buying and Selling

Everywhere people are making, selling, buying and distributing goods. Commerce and industry together create changing patterns in the landscape.

Commerce simply means exchanging things that people need. This can be raw materials, such as wool or cotton, or finished articles, such as clothing. It can be ore from which metal is extracted; machine parts made from the metal; or machines themselves.

Industry is not just manufacturing goods in a factory. It is work done by 'industrious' people. Anyone who works for a living is involved in industry.

People work at getting fish from the sea, or oil from the earth. This is **primary industry**. Some use materials to make a finished product, this is **manufacturing industry**. Others, like waiters and dentists, work to provide service for others. This is **service industry**.

Oil is found deep under the sea bed. It is extracted, refined and then distributed all over the world. ▼

Simple commerce is usually carried out at a place set aside for that purpose. Once, most people brought produce to a market place and sold it themselves. Now many goods can be moved rapidly by road, rail, or ship. So a farmer or manufacturer may sell in bulk to a single person or company. They, in turn, sell farm produce or manufactured goods to shops or other factories.

Demands for Produce

Commerce and industry can completely change a rural landscape. Some commodities, like sugar, are needed world-wide. So in the West Indies and Fiji, for example, sugar cane fields have replaced tropical vegetation.

▲ Special depots like this, in Sydney harbour, are set up in many ports, so that container ships can rapidly load and unload cargo packed into these standard-size metal boxes (containers).

Sugar cane, grown in great quantities in plantations in the West Indies and Fiji. ▼

Industries and Landscape

The effect of industry depends on its scale. The family-owned brickworks in Sri Lanka has resulted in a new landscape of small clay-pits and ponds amid the rubber trees and palms. ▼

Everyone needs clothing. As a result, huge inland areas in Australia are grazed by sheep to provide wool. Sheep pens, shearing- and packing-sheds are part of the scenery. Similarly, land in China and India is transformed by cotton-growing. Many people are involved in the growing, packing and transporting.

However, making textiles and cotton clothing takes place at very different levels. Hand-looms can be set up in small workshops, amid local buildings. But large textile factories create industrial scenery.

Factories are usually grouped together near a source of energy or where materials are obtained locally or through a port.

The industrial landscape is made up of factories, workers' houses, power stations, roads and railways. It changes when new processes require new buildings; or as demands for a product increase or decrease.

Raw Materials
Where minerals are extracted, effects on landscape also depend on scale. A Sri Lankan family brick-making business depends on hand-digging clay from small pits and drying it in the sun. Great mechanical grabs removing

A cotton boll

brick-clay in Bedfordshire cut deep into farmland. Though the old pits are filled and reclaimed, the tall, smoking chimneys, brickworks and dumps stand out.

Often the countryside affected is far from the centre of industry. Huge stretches of Canadian forest are continually being cut and replaced. Wood is pulped to paper for the world's daily newspapers.

▲ The demands for the fibre from the cotton ball formed by the flower have caused huge areas to become cotton plantations and for distant cotton mills to create an industrial landscape.

Here in Canada the heavy raw material, soft-wood logs, is floated and poled directly to the nearby factory, changing the ◄ natural landscape.

Did You Know?

There are 3 main types of industry:

● Primary industry (which includes farming, mining, forestry and fishing);

● Secondary industry (which means all the manufacturing industries);

● Tertiary industry (which means all the service industries, such as catering and tourism, the armed forces, hospitals and fire fighting.

Different Industries

Metal ores, coking coal, and other minerals may be transformed by energy and labour into metals, and then to heavy products such as steel girders. ▼

Manufacturing industries are not all alike. **Heavy industries**, like iron and steel, use large amounts of heavy raw materials. They make bulky products and take up large areas of land.

Light industries use less bulky materials. They make lighter products. Factories making furniture, processing foods, or printing are usually more compact. They can be specially sited near transport routes, or set up in planned **industrial estates**.

Some light industries involve the use of **high technology**. Many are connected with electronics: TV parts, computers, scientific instruments, for example. They are often grouped together in what are termed 'hi-tech parks'.

They will have close links with other 'hi-tech' industries and research centres. These may be based in another country. So a site near a motorway, or close to an airport, is an advantage.

Industrial landscapes, therefore, vary a great deal. Large cities provide both customers and workers. Most have industrial districts with a maze of factories, transport yards, offices and communications. A particular industry may have special effects on the

Heavy industry

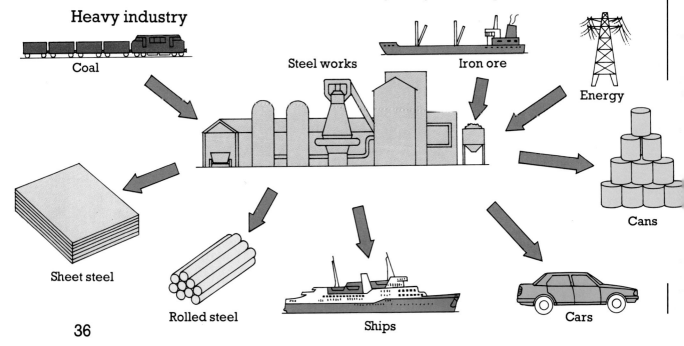

Coal

Steel works

Iron ore

Energy

Sheet steel

Rolled steel

Ships

Cans

Cars

scenery. Oil-refining and chemical works need to be kept away from towns. Many are sited near deep water, and clash with scenic landscapes. Even those inland, served by pipelines, stand out in the landscape, and can be **pollution** hazards.

Some industries use energy and labour to transform less bulky raw or manufactured materials into light products. ▼

Light industry

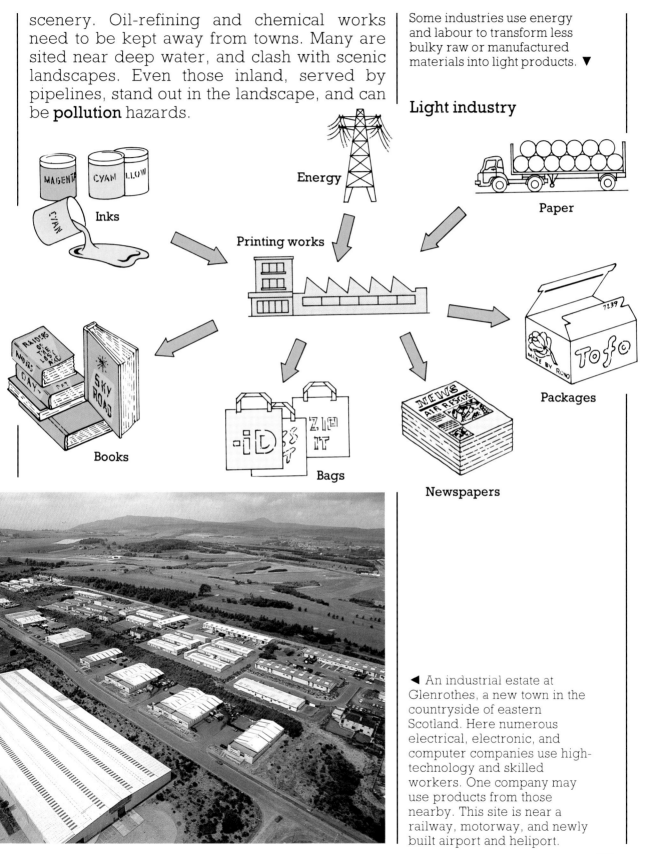

Inks

Energy

Paper

Printing works

Books

Bags

Newspapers

Packages

◀ An industrial estate at Glenrothes, a new town in the countryside of eastern Scotland. Here numerous electrical, electronic, and computer companies use high-technology and skilled workers. One company may use products from those nearby. This site is near a railway, motorway, and newly built airport and heliport.

Big Business

Some commodities are sold direct from farm, quarry or factory to the people who want them. But other commodities may be moved in bulk from country to country. Buying and selling, and planning the movement of goods from one country to another, takes place in offices, far from where they are produced.

Big cities have a central district where many offices are linked by telephone and computer to those in other countries. They agree the prices of the goods that are traded between them. The goods must be insured and transported. So here too are insurance and transport offices.

The business of buying and selling therefore creates a distinctive landscape. Commercial buildings in the heart of a city will overlook a scene of trade, transport and industry.

Industry and Commerce

Some cities have business centres where people from many countries arrange to exchange commodities and foreign money. Hong Kong has one. It is situated where Pacific trade routes meet. In 1997 it will be restored to

The central business district of Toronto, looking inland from Lake Ontario. ▼

◄ Light industry and business offices are often built on the edges of larger towns and cities. This means that goods, people and service equipment can come and go with relative ease, avoiding the congested city centres.

The People's Republic of China, as a remarkable combination of industry and commerce.

It is noted for numerous small industries. Its clothing, electronic goods, jewellery and other products are sold in thousands of small shops. The offices of international firms produce a spectacular **high-rise landscape.**

As populations grow and demand new things, so the landscapes created by commerce and industry are always changing.

Toronto's central business district, whose high-rise banks, insurance firms, offices and stores serve one another as well as the public. Much of the small old inner housing has been cleared. Most people live further out. But workers in offices, in the old clothing firms, or newer dockside industries (p. 45) must travel in daily. There is well-planned public transport. ▼

Residential area

Business area

Clothing firms

6: TRANSPORT

Simple Forms of Transport

Rough tracks, footpaths, and stone-paved roads have linked one place to another ever since people began to live in settlements. In many parts of the world goods are still carried on the head or shoulders, strapped to animals, or pushed or pulled in carts.

Pack animals are in everyday use in many countries. They carry produce to and from scattered fields, returning each day with fodder gleaned from the countryside. They are able to follow rough paths up rocky hill-sides and tracks through woodland. Camel trains still carry loads long distances across the Sahara. Yaks and pack horses transport goods over the stony deserts of Central Asia.

In the more closely settled parts of the less developed countries, roads have been improved, but animal transport is cheaper than powered vehicles. In India the ox-cart is still widely used.

▲ A Roman pavement, linking one remote valley with another in a mountainous and wild part of North Wales. The large slabs of flat stone were placed in a line to give the soldiers a reasonable route.

In southern Germany a river valley runs (left to right) through the wooded hills. It is joined by tributary valleys; each followed by a road. So here a route centre has developed on both sides of the river. ▶

In most Chinese towns the market is a throng of push-carts, cycle carriers, horse-drawn vehicles, and oil-powered tractors and trailers.

Pack horses are still the best ▲ form of transport for the nomadic Kirghiz who travel through barren, stony mountainous country bordering eastern China.

The Market Pattern of Roads

We have seen how in rural areas a well-sited town may become a central market. Well-used roads from the surrounding villages form one pattern and as the town itself grows the regular roads of spreading suburbs appear on the landscape as well.

With modern transport, market towns now depend on well-surfaced roads. For instance, people from remote areas in high valleys in the Andes depend on public transport using good roads. The people are mostly from mountain villages. They carry their bundles to and from the main road, and pack into a bus going to the weekly market.

Canals

The Bridgewater Canal

The Industrial Revolution started in Great Britain at the end of the eighteenth century. One of the first forms of transport used to move heavy raw materials, like coal and iron ore, to feed the growing industries, were barges. To help them move from place to place, special canals were built. Probably the earliest of importance was the Bridgewater Canal, built between Worsley and Manchester in 1761.

Long ago people dug canals for boats to carry bulky materials. Two of China's great rivers, which carry goods from west to east, were linked by a north-south canal over 200 years BC. For hundreds of years the canals that were dug in The Netherlands to drain the land have also been used for transport.

Today roads and railways have made small inland canals less important for carrying goods. But large canals connecting inland waters to the sea are still important, for instance in America, where the Great Lakes are used by large freight vessels. In 1985, a new canal opened up hundreds of kilometres of waterways from the Tennessee river to the Gulf of Mexico. This new north-south route, running alongside the Mississippi, carries millions of tonnes of freight a year.

Inland Waterways and Ports

Water is still a cheap way of carrying freight. Canals, like the Suez and Panama, cut through necks of land to link oceans for large vessels. A river, such as the Rhine, can be a valuable transport route between sea ports and inland manufacturing areas.

The Tennessee-Tombigbee rivers are linked to give an ocean outlet for grain, coal and lumber. ▶

The Rhine serves many industrial regions, from its broad delta in The Netherlands to Switzerland. Docks at Rotterdam and Euro-poort transfer goods between ocean ships and the powered barges that travel up and down the Rhine.

In many places factories, refineries, and chemical works lie along the river banks. Road and rail traffic also follow the river itself.

▲ For centuries the Dutch have used canal systems to drain the coastal lowlands and for communications. They also harnessed the energy of the wind, using windmills.

Rotterdam at the mouth of the Rhine. Here ocean shipping exchanges freight with land transport and barges plying Europe's inland waterways. ▼

◄ A ship in the Panama Canal approaches the locks which control this link between the Pacific Ocean and the Caribbean.

Transport Networks

Ocean traffic affects the landscape at the docks. There are road and rail transport terminals for freight and passengers. There are warehouses, or space for stacking and loading **containers**.

Major land routes may have surprisingly little effect on the countryside. Railways are often hidden in cuttings. Motorways help take traffic away from minor roads and small towns. They frequently give good views of open country.

Where they meet, at ports or cities, routeways cover the landscape.

Where Routes Meet

Passengers and goods are continuously transported in and out of big cities. Many are transferred from one terminal near the city centre to another – from train to road vehicle, or to shipping at a port.

Apart from the main routeways, the countryside is covered with networks of smaller ones. Rail transport runs along fixed routes. A single train can carry many passengers and much freight. A road vehicle

Traffic along road, rail and canal meet at Amsterdam's central station. This canal now provides local transport; but waterways still link the great port to the North Sea. ▶

carries less, but can run both on main roads and minor ones, and serve a wide area.

Many goods are now carried in standard containers. They are easy to pack; and time is saved in handling a single container. They are easily transferred between ship, road and rail transport. Large firms set up transport depots, where the contents of large containers are split up. Road vehicles then supply widespread shops and shopping centres.

▲ Toronto's harbour on Lake Ontario with its inter-connected transport systems. Notice the docks, dockside roads, the motorway and numerous car parks, the rail lines and shipping.

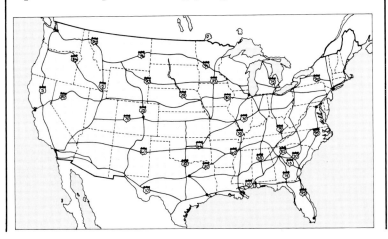

◀ A map of the United States of America, showing all the States (marked by a dotted line) and the main roads that cross the country linking them up. The numbers of the roads (or highways, as the Americans call them) are also shown. These roads are used by the public and also by large haulage lorries that carry goods from one place to another.

Some Bad Effects

Congested roads in cities throughout the world are a common sight. Solutions to this problem have been looked for but there seems to be no easy answer to this modern hazard. Land in cities is scarce and expensive, so building more and bigger roads is not a simple scheme. ▼

People in the developed countries have the advantage of advanced forms of transport. They cannot live without modern vehicles and communications. Unfortunately most forms of transport and communications have their drawbacks.

At rush hours, main roads are congested with traffic. Too often they are part of hideous urban scenery. Road signs, wires, cables, advertising posters, together make a dreary urban or suburban landscape. Traffic fumes add to air pollution.

Airports occupy huge areas of countryside beyond the big cities. They are linked to the cities by rapid road and rail transport. But the noise of aircraft disturbs people nearby, and room must be found for the airport hotels and car parks, and for service areas for the planes.

Other Communications

Communications include instant means of contact, like the telephone, telex, radio and television. Aerials, wires and cables form a 'wirescape' in many towns. Groups of large white 'dishes' to receive signals from communications satellites can be found in many developed countries. Many households now have small dish receivers to pick up long-distance television signals.

These valuable forms of instant communication are linked with transport on land, sea and air. In Australia, radio and air transport combine to create a life-saving service for remote families.

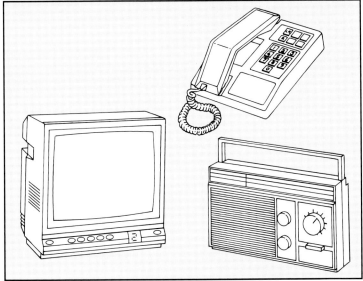

◀ Traffic, dominated by yellow cabs, pours into New York's Times Square; pedestrians throng pavements, garish signs thrust consumer goods at the public.

A roof-top view of inner city housing points to the means of instant communication which are now household articles in industrially developed countries, like those opposite. ▼

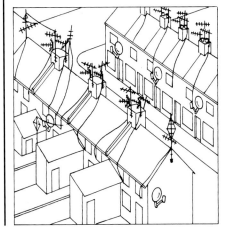

7: LANDSCAPE UNDER PRESSURE

Over-population

By the year 2000 there will be over six thousand million people living in the world. The greatest growth is still in the less developed countries. Here over-population first affects rural families who do not have enough land to support themselves. Many move to the overcrowded cities, but few are able to find jobs.

People with Nowhere to Go

In some developed countries people have escaped overcrowding by emigrating. Many found fertile farmland overseas, or worked in forestry or mining, often in the homeland of other people.

The map shows the high rate of population growth in the less developed countries. The graph shows how better health and a longer life has caused world population to soar. ▼

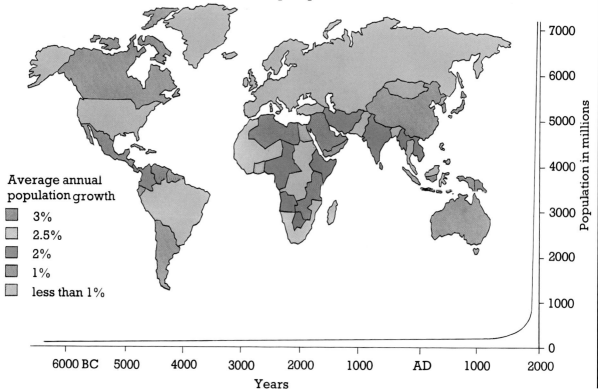

Average annual population growth

- 3%
- 2.5%
- 2%
- 1%
- less than 1%

In Paraguay, numerous Amer-Indian families lived amid the Chaco's grassy woodland; until European settlers from eastern Paraguay extended farming and timber cutting westwards. Many displaced tribal people now have an 'in-between' life, no longer supporting themselves in the Chaco, and with no place in urban life. They live in shack housing near the capital, Ascunción. There are many displaced peoples of this kind – Aborigines in Australia; Bushmen in Africa's Kalahari desert.

▲ Increasing population in a small area results in high-rise housing packed with families crammed into a few rooms – as here in Hong Kong, where the washing lines indicate the numbers involved.

More Factories, More Waste

Increasing demands for manufactures can harm the landscape, for factories produce waste. Chimneys release smoke and gases high in the air, where wind should disperse them. Yet air conditions sometimes cause local pollution. Sinking air can trap fumes close to the ground. It also keeps away rain clouds.

In some places the air sinks most of the time. It causes desert conditions in coastal Peru, where the capital city of Lima must rely on mountain waters. The rapidly growing population causes water shortages.

The Disposable Society

The rubbish of the rich is sifted by the poor in this South American city. They are looking for things of use, that they can repair or sell. ▼

Demands for the latest products also put pressure on the landscape. Manufacturers persuade us to discard old goods and buy new ones. Natural resources are rapidly used up. Not only do factories pollute the environment, but we foul it with 'throw-aways'. Yet many things we demand are luxuries in a world where millions are short of basic foods and materials.

Industries also pollute rivers, for a riverside site can be an advantage. Even large rivers such as the Rhine become 'chemical sewers'. These chemicals are usually invisible; but the smell from the Rhine drifts far from the river.

Farm fertilisers also pollute water. When washed into rivers and lakes, they feed small water organisms such as algae. Dense green masses of plants form, which take oxygen from the water. Fish and other life-forms perish.

Did You Know?

● Europe and North America together use as much artificial fertilizer as the rest of the world put together.

● An average person in the USA produces over 700 kg of domestic waste every year.

● Over half the aluminium cans produced in the USA for drinks are today recycled – a step in the right direction.

◀ Packaging adds to daily costs and the problems of getting rid of the wastes.

Factories pour chemical wastes into the middle Rhine, and continuous barge traffic adds to pollution – all the result of increasing demand for industrial products. ▼

The Natural World

Nowadays people travel far to admire the natural landscape and wildlife. But they seldom appreciate how easily the natural balance is upset.

A shepherd and his sheep on a Mediterranean hillside hardly seem to threaten the landscape. But grazing removes sparse vegetation from thin, dry soils. Overgrazing causes serious erosion.

Tourists themselves pollute the sights they come to see. Hotels disrupt fine landscapes. People leave litter. They bring diseases into

This goatherd lives in Turkey, near the Mediterranean coast. His flock includes a few sheep amongst the goats. Both types of animal remove the sparse vegetation from the thin, dry soils by chewing grass down to the roots. The result can be increasing infertile, semi-desert land. ▼

game areas. Their vehicles cut tracks. They turn wildlife habitats into open zoos.

Fire can be harmful. Farmers burn off old vegetation to help new shoots develop. But careless fires destroy vast areas of tree plantations each year, and sweep across dry farmlands. During dry periods, Australian states ban fires in agricultural areas.

The demands for more farmland threaten natural landscapes. 'Wetlands' seem unattractive to many people and enormous areas are drained each year. Yet they are habitats for birds, animals, fish and insects adapted to marsh conditions. They also support migrant birds.

Relandscaping

Both rural land uses and spreading industrial sites put enormous strain on the landscape. Where old industries have declined and vanished, the dumps and tips they left behind often have not. A recent move in some countries has been to turn these areas into gardens and parks by spending time and money landscaping them. This can change depressing examples of rural destruction into landscapes to enjoy.

▲ What was once an unsightly waste tip in Germany's industrial Ruhr has been turned into a pleasant park for young and old alike.

Wetlands are very important natural habitats for many different species of wildlife. They are under threat from developers who want to build on them. It is important to make sure that the wetlands do not disappear entirely. ▼

8: KNOWING WHAT IS HAPPENING

Local Problems

We have seen many examples of landscapes being changed in unpleasant or harmful ways. Sometimes people are careless about pollution. Sometimes circumstances such as over-population and drought cause damage.

Even when people try to improve conditions, they may end up by making them worse. Families moved from poor, old housing into new high-rise flats have often felt trapped in rooms far above street life and playgrounds. We need to understand why towns should have planned landscapes.

Planners can record details of land use in urban areas from the town centre to the outer suburbs. Street maps from the town planning department can be used to record what each building is used for – a ground-floor shop with

High-rise flats rise from the small terrace houses clustered about the old factories: but do new high flats suit family life better than old ground-level housing? ▼

offices or flats above, perhaps. Many will be private houses.

The results can help us to understand patterns within a town. We can see why urban changes are necessary, and consider, for example, why houses close to the town centre are being replaced by tall office blocks. We can make towns more pleasant to live in.

Similarly, rural fieldwork can make us aware of the balance between natural vegetation, soils and crops.

A Scientific Approach

Scientific research improves farming landscapes and can introduce new methods to replace old unsuitable ones. For instance, planting one crop between another is both profitable and helps prevent soil erosion.

A scientific wildlife study can ensure that endangered species are given a safe natural environment in which they can develop.

Ordinary people are not always aware of what is going on about them. Careful checking is needed to look after people's interests.

◄ The key to providing a better urban environment is careful planning. The surveyor (below) helps to prepare maps of houses, roads, and gardens like that on the left. But others must consider whether the buildings and lay-out are suitable for family life, provide parks and recreation areas, and check environmental pollution.

A land surveyor

Theodolite
(an instrument used by surveyors for measuring angles on the Earth's surface)

A View from Space

Scientists must have reliable information from which to devise ways of conserving or developing the landscape. To see exactly what is happening over the Earth's surface from day to day is obviously a tremendous task. Aircraft and satellites now provide views from space and abundant information about weather, soils, vegetation, oceans and people's activities.

Thousands of artificial objects now encircle the earth. Some are used for communications; many observe the earth's surface. They allow a study of weather and surface conditions; and give warnings of hurricanes, forest fires, or locust swarms.

Satellites

Satellites **orbit** high above the Earth, far enough out in the atmosphere to avoid being pulled back down again or burned up by friction with the air. Some communications satellites are designed to move in orbit at the same rate that the Earth turns beneath them. This means that they stay over the same spot on the Earth's surface.

Facts and Feats

● A satellite stationed 160 km (100 miles) above Earth can be so accurate in taking a photograph that it could read the words on this page.

● Weather satellites have been in orbit around Earth since 1960. They have helped to predict the onslaught of bad weather and have no doubt saved many lives in the process.

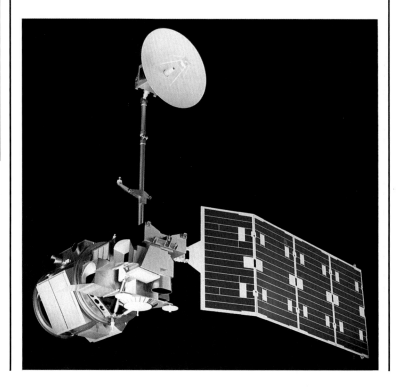

The Landsat-D satellite receives and transmits information about vegetation, land-use, mineral and water resources. ▶

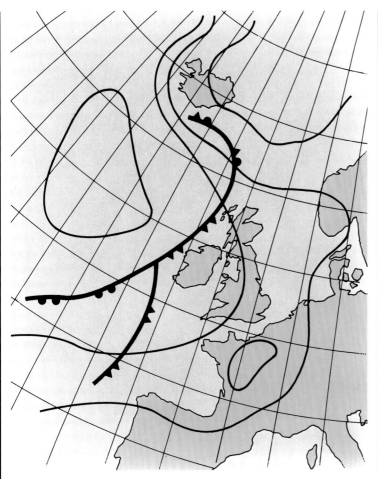

Geostationary Orbits

Some satellites move at the speed the Earth rotates and in the same direction. This means that they always remain above the same spot on the Earth's surface. To do this successfully, they must also be at least 35,680 km (22,300 miles) above the Earth. When this is so, they are said to be in a geostationary orbit.

◀ This map tells us what weather to expect over a period of a few days. Satellite information helps meteorologists build up a more accurate picture of weather patterns than was previously possible.

Data received by a ground-scanning satellite build up a mosaic of images of the entire surface of the USA. Various colours and tones are used to show water and different land surfaces. ▼

Landsat

Satellites orbiting the Earth relay information that help us to understand better the world in which we live. ▶

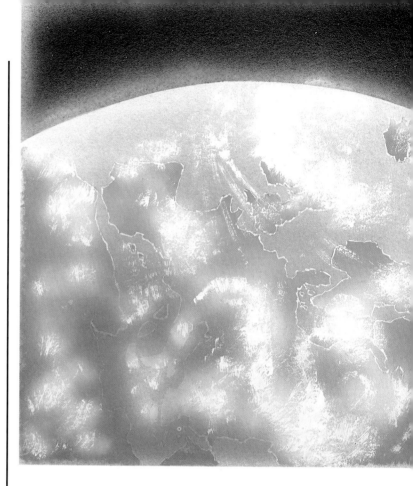

Keeping an Eye on the World

The **Landsat satellites** orbit the Earth, recording a variety of information. This includes:

- distinguishing species of vegetation;

- measuring pollution in water;

- recording plant matter levels in water;

- measuring moisture levels in soil and vegetation;

- cloud and snow observation;

- identifying rock types;

- measuring heat from various surfaces.

Other types of satellites are made specially to sense weather conditions and monitor ocean resources.

Satellites such as Landsat encircle the Earth from the North Pole to the South Pole (a polar orbit). As the Earth turns beneath the satellite, it will be able to scan the surface.

The latest Landsat orbits the Earth once every 99 minutes and scans almost the whole surface every 16 days.

Each picture it takes shows an area 185 by 185 km (115 miles). It senses light and heat wavelengths, which enable us to distinguish different types of rock, soil and vegetation (even plant matter in the seas) and to compare the temperatures of surface features.

Observing Landscape Changes

Such scanning enables us to check the surface very carefully. Heat changes in the area near the volcano Vesuvius where the farmlands and the city of Naples are threatened by volcanic activity, can be continuously observed.

Changes between desert features, land use in irrigated areas, water control, and urban

spread could be monitored in detail at regular intervals.

Thus many features of our changing landscapes can be brought to notice in time for us to deal with them if need be. Whether the people who occupy the area concerned would have the knowledge or resources to prevent disasters is another matter.

◄ Here data received by a Landsat-4 satellite above Vesuvius and the Bay of Naples have been used to build up false colour images. Overall they show the contrasts between urban areas (green) and natural vegetation and crops in various tones of red. Notice the road patterns and the clear relief of the great volcano and the other craters (left) beyond the city.

59

Glossary

Acid rain: fumes from factories and power stations, which contain oxides of sulphur and nitrogen, form acids with water vapour. These fall as rain and make it difficult for some forms of life to survive.

Atmosphere the envelope of various gases (including hydrogen and oxygen) that surrounds the Earth.

Battery hens: large numbers of birds caged under artificial conditions, with automatic feeding, cleaning and egg collection.

Carbohydrate: a compound made up of carbon, hydrogen and oxygen, like the starches and sugar formed by plants.

Collective group: people who work together as a community and share the results of their planning and labour.

Colonial port: a port once set up as a trade base by foreigners occupying a country; often to send raw materials from the colony to their homelands.

Community: a group of people living close to one another and sharing interests.

Container: a box of standard size which can be packed with goods and easily stacked and transferred from one form of transport to another.

Crop rotation: planting a crop which can return to the soil chemicals which the previous crop has removed; part of a planned sequence of crops over the years.

Crustal plate: one of the segments into which the solid part of the Earth's surface is divided. It is slowly moved by molten material beneath.

Delta: a certain type of river mouth, that has spread out to make a fan shape due to silt deposits carried by the river.

Ecosystem: a balanced community of plants, animals and non-living things sharing a particular environment.

Environment: all the physical features, climate and living forms which are found in a particular area.

Erosion: the process by which landscapes are slowly changed. They are eaten away by the action of rain, wind and ice.

Extensive farming: a method of farming a large area by spending little and employing few people.

Factory farm: a well-organised farm, like a factory, where much is spent on materials and energy to grow and process high quality produce.

Fertile: something (an animal, plant or the soil, for instance) is said to be fertile when it is able to reproduce itself, to bear seeds or to produce babies.

Grain elevator: a large building designed to store grain which is lifted up, or sucked up, from rail- or road-trucks.

Gravity: the force of attraction which exists between the Earth and other bodies, which are pulled towards the centre of the Earth.

Harrow: a tool used to break up top-soil and clods of earth.

Heavy industry: a type of industry which produces goods which are heavy and usually bulky.

Hide: the skin of an animal, often used by people as a covering or to make clothing.

High-rise landscape: a landscape with tall buildings with many storeys:

High technology: technology which uses scientific methods, often with electronic components.

Industrial estate: an area with buildings, water supply, power-lines and car parks laid out for light industries to use.

Intensive farming: a method of farming where a large amount of money is spent on machinery and fertilisers and where many people work to produce goods for the market.

Landmass: a broad land area or continent; in contrast to oceans and smaller islands.

Landsat satellite: first launched by NASA (US) in 1972 to transmit information about the Earth's surface to ground stations; a series of satellites has followed.

Life expectancy: the years a person may expect to live from birth, or from a particular age.

Light industry: one in which both the materials used and the products are relatively light.

Mahogany: a rainforest tree with a hard reddish-brown wood, much used for furniture.

Manufacturing industry: one which processes or assembles materials to form a finished product.

Orbit: the path an object takes going round another object. For example, the Moon orbits the Earth, the Earth orbits the sun. A rocket may orbit a planet.

Pesticide: a chemical substance used to kill pests, such as harmful insects.

Plant species: plants belonging to the same family that have certain characteristics in common.

Pollution: a way in which people foul their environment.

Primary industry: getting things from natural resources, but not processing them; the processing is *secondary industry*.

Sapodilla: a rainforest tree from which an elastic gum is tapped to use in making chewing gum.

Service industry: one that provides a service (like banking) rather than manufacturing things.

Solar energy: short-wave radiation from the Sun, which provides heat and light, and energy for plant growth.

Suburbs: the outskirts of a town or city. Suburbs are areas where people live rather than work.

Virus: minute forms which grow in cells of living creatures and cause disease.

Weathering: the way rocks crack, split or peel when exposed to weather elements such as wind, frost and acid rainwater.

Index

A **Bold** number shows the entry is illustrated on that page. The same page often has writing about the entry too.